Signpost to Via Lucis

Poetry on the Radiance of the Resurrection

by

Joe Bisicchia

This array is for you to take in but not to individually hold. As light of the world, we are each a signpost made to reflect our faith, to follow our Lord through grace, and to share the Way of the Light. Shine onward!

Contents

Signpost 7

Maker of the Light 8

Rise Your Star 9

At Your Manger 10

At Your Cross 11

Cross of Victory 12

Risen 13

Today's Good News 14

Rising From the Dead 15

Darkness 16

Empty Tomb 17

We're Sheep 18

Let There Be Light 19

As for Death 20

The Risen Lord Appears 21

Thy Name 22

Harmony Within Stained Glass 23

Sound of Light 24

See a Choir of Angels 25

Bramble on the Cold Hill 26

Persistence of Light 27

Rapid Eye Movement 28

Morning Walk 29

windows on the way 30

While on the Everyday Way 31

King of Radiant Glory 32

The Wise 33

We Are Here 34

Prayers Within Windows 35

Wick Within the Wax 36

In the Breaking of the Bread 37

And When the Wick Withers 38

Within Awe 39

Sunshine Upon Our Foyer 40

Like Lilies Love Light 41

Walking Back From Emmaus 42

Living Like Psalm 23 43

Acts of the Apostles 44

Vibrant Field of Blossom 45

Power of Peace 46

This Way of Light 47

Puzzle Peace 48

Peace Talks 49

True Colors 50

Of the Marks We Leave 51

Prayer for Faith in the Dark 52

Love Never Dies 53

Without Faith, We Cannot Survive 54

Love Is to *See* and Believe 55

Wounds of the Living 56

Moonrise Over the Sea 57

No Need to Worry 58

Living the Living 59

Our Everyday Place 60

Gathering of Stars 61

To Shepherd Us 62

Do You Love Me? 63

Act of God, Act of Love 64

And Forth We Are Sent 65

Love Ascends and Stays 66

Your Light Shows the Way 67

Sky Lanterns 68

Sometimes It's Just Overcast 69

Presence of God 70

Depth of Self 71

Nimbus of Us 72

We All Know Hope 73
Holy Spirit 74
Spirit, Breathe 75
And Who Are We? 76
We Are the Light of the World 77
Lighthouse 78
Inexhaustible 79
Light Beams 80
Light-Bearers 81
Light Carries Us 82
Fireflies, Our Souls 83
Ray of Light 84
Streams the Light 85
Via Lucis 86

Signpost

Sign of the cross, and here we are.

Fellow traveler, this is you and this is me.
Now a signpost, each.
In life's journey of signposts.

What does yours say?
Better yet, how well do I read?
It's a readable font, vivid on the highway
or back alley if one opens eye to see.

Let it be Good News for it to say:

Via Lucis.
Way of the Light.

As for me, you have the better view.
Tell me, is there connection as I speak?
Let it be the same Good News
for those in the dark night of the soul.

Good News, for where there is darkness,
light.

Let it be, for both you and me, a start
of a poetry collection
with the most important question—

Who do we see?

Maker of the Light

In the beginning was the Word,
and the Word was with God.

In the beginning, Love was and is.
And shall forever be.
I Am is Love.

In the beginning, as divinely writ,
God created the heavens and the earth
and the earth was without form or shape.

"Let there be light."
There is light.
It shines in the darkness,
and the darkness shall not overcome it.

Through Him all things were made.
In Him there is life,
and that life is the light of all mankind.

Now, we have the choice to see.
To choose the light or the darkness.

"What do you want me to do for you?"
Jesus asks.

Surely there is the light for you to see.
Waiting.
So, Whom are you looking for?

Rise Your Star

Lord, help us see You.

Help us find our eyes.
Our souls need Your light.
Seems, in the blindness of night
we sometimes toss them away.

Help us Your manger to find.
Lord, find us there clear as day.
Near as here.
Here, where You are.

You make the path straight,
this way of living, this land, this life.
Station to station we follow.
You are the way.

You've brought us here
from Ur of the Chaldeans
to here, from the Wadi of Egypt
to the Great River, the Euphrates,

following Your light.

At Your Manger

At an everyday place.
Even mirrored, an everyday face.
Everywhere in the world by grace.
A sign wide as all of light.

We fall at Your transfiguration.
Divine to human, ever Divine.
To be disfigured in Your Passion.
Arrayed in your Resurrection.

And now, here we are.

Our human senses pale.
Let us hear without ears,
see without eyes,
touch as only a soul to soul can.

And be cradled.

Help us all, everywhere,
to allow ourselves the Light
despite obstacles, blockages,
things in the way, so to be this:

Yours.

The miracle upon us every day.

At Your Cross

We had wandered far from Love
amidst a world far from grace,
tight to earth's fleeting premises,
like nail to wood,
survival of the fittest,
and all its broken promises.

And here we are now
seeing the right hand of God.
You save us through the Cross.
Here, where hearts reach.
Here, where hallowed be Thy Name.
Here, where mercy is near.

This very day shall be paradise,
for heaven has shown the way.
Even as Your hands are nailed back,
You take us into Your arms,
for nothing can hold back
Love's embrace.

Cross of Victory

Within the fallen pomegranate,
and all that is life, is now,
not just in the seed, but foremost
at the start in the Sacred Heart
as so conceived. We are of God.

God is. As Love is. Inexplicably,
simply,
is.

Pain had a way of permanence
and yet no longer. Chasm of darkness
can be deep, but it is defeated.
Love completes us, not death.
Love has no end.

See the Cross, now in the distance,
but not forgotten.
See the price God has paid for us
with Love begotten.

Yes, so to endlessly enfold us,
God has spread His arms.

Risen

Even as
the March frost carves the prism
strands upon the waiting grass,
even as summer's heat ripples
Main Street to a froth,
even as the peppered leaves leap
from no longer adorned trees,
even as
the air fills the lung with the brush
of Christmas,
the choir sings this early Easter morn,
bird by bird,
from the womb, orbs of color,
extraordinary things and wings,
all that lifts from the tomb,
hallelujah, hallelujah, hallelujah!

This newborn day is of forever.

Today.

Now, see all that we are.

Today's Good News

We are here.

That is the *where* of our lives.

Fellow pilgrims,
we are on the Way of Light,
this Via Lucis.

This is not about
accomplishing a distance.

This is surrendering to here.
With endless joy.
To God's presence.
A priceless gift.

This is all within the soul,
all the life that we are to live.
To give.

This is the purpose of life,
the *who* and *why* we are.
This is all our existence.

Rising From the Dead

All of us shall die.
Each and every single one.
No mortal life is spared,
for we each will have our time.

And today,
we make our way in the dark,
but how?

By God.

The Risen Lord is not dead,
but beyond death.
The architect of Love has no end.
Thus, Love has no end.
This Love is our Shepherd.
God is light years beyond any limits.
Beyond time.
And thus, too,
we are beyond time.

We are of God.

See our God-given salvation
as eternity,
this Way of Light.

In the current, we move ahead.
Here where we timelessly are.

Darkness

No heart should be buried aside the brush,
in a soul's blindness, paved with hate.
So it is when allowing the evil one to invade,
wiping away all that is good, all that is light.

Darkness can seem to draw more near.
But light wipes away the dark.
Here we are, light years in speed and
Who hears each heartbeat into outer space?

No need to linger or languish in loneliness,
in sin, lost.
No matter the depth, salvation is not far away.
It is here, sprung forth from the Cross.

Floodlit we now are, here on our daily way.
Here is the Way of Light, station to station.
If only we open the skylights of the heart.
If only we allow our inner eye to see.

See, yes, Love.
And be.
Even as the tomb seems impenetrable
in the dark.

Empty Tomb

Our Savior formed us from clay,
envisioned us as Love, as God is.
Made us in that Divine image.

Here we all are,
each a precious being upon this
shared stone earth that spins on its axis.

Here we all are
in our varying degrees of emptiness,
some so alone, so outcast, so far apart.

Here we all are, hiding in our silos
of loneliness, where face and face
are too often leper and leper.

Here we all are, and God knows us,
suffers for us, and is with each of us,
all of us in the dark.

Look and see, and know,
the Angel of the Lord says,
"Do not be afraid! After all,

Who is it that we seek?"

None of us is to be alone.
Open your eyes and see.
The Lord has rolled away the stone.

We're Sheep

We're sheep now rising from sleep.
Even in the darkness, able to fully see.
This is you and me set to believe.

This is like the star in Bethlehem
showing where we now are.
Providing epiphany.

This is INRI and all its majesty.

And we follow.

This is life,
no longer an empty tomb of night.

This is the present ongoing path,
where we are,
now.

Alive.

Let There Be Light

No divide, no separation.
We are Parthians, Medes, and Elamites,
inhabitants of Mesopotamia, Judea and

the whole world.

And see, darkness covers the earth.
But no longer.

Darkness covers far too many a heart.
Prodigal we are.
But no longer.

Who waits for us at the horizon?

Who is stronger than death?

We can move mountains out of the way.
We can recognize the Face.
Who knows you, as you are?

The way through darkness is faith.

The defeater of death is Christ.

Every day is a new station on the way
in the never-ending gift
of Love's intrepid presence.

Full of grace.
We stream onward.

As for Death

We can now leave it behind.
Its sting.
Death has been defeated.

No accomplishment on our own.
No award to single us out.
Just an immeasurable gift of God.

Now, what shall we become?
You and I are surely not alone.
We are fully loved and fully known.

Let us be life.
All of its glory.
Stars of God's light.

The Risen Lord Appears

Eyes of faith witness the majesty of God's Light. Recognition is awareness. Dignity. Proximity. Despite all ignorance, epiphany. Plain as prayer. Heard near as here. We are called by name. Such wonder in the Name. Never in vain. Not one shouted to defame. Ever Light, even in seemingly impenetrable gloom.

Frail not, the Light. The Name exists pure as that Light. Colors, prism, fire erasing the blankness. Same as Burning Bush. Moses wanted to know the Name, so to share. I AM. For God is. And God is everywhere.

Should not be hard to find.

We all are here in God's image. Wondrously made by God. Loved by Love. There is power in recognition. There is receipt. We are made to recognize each other in the Light. To see God as Love. See with all our senses. Love calls us by name. We share a world of names. All around are faces seen. More unseen. Names upon names unknown. Too many seemingly solved as numbers or as labels cruelly engraved. Too many purposely unnamed by others, forgotten, tossed to the side, ignored. But meant for the Light. Love calls us by name. Each with a name. Each with a soul. Each needing the Good News. To share it. Not to just hold it within, under a bushel.

Light is not to be hidden.

This life to live, this road, the Way of Light, is where God is, and where we are called to be. Signposts. Each a Sign of the Cross.

Thy Name

Lovelier than the morning carolers,
more powerful than any bluster
or rushed train or wind's brush.
All is pale in comparison to You.

New as the day is new, Thy Name.
Let us lift our horns not in vain
but in undeniable faith, a clarity
as a whispered child to mother,

as elsewhere dying breath to sky,
as grace before breaking bread,
as lover-to-lover souls together,
as prayer through the air to Love.

So it is to love
who was and is and shall be Love,
as entwined as one in our breasts
as we rise from our nests and hear.

You beckon our own names.
Not one of us to fall without You
ever near, our rescue.
Abba, we love You.

May we venerate You as Love
through our lives in the light,
expressed in all we do
as Love, just the same.

Harmony Within Stained Glass

Eyes wide.
Canyons of landscape to the light.

Rays of Easter morn.
And then, vibrant green again to soon sing.

To some outsiders, it is distant and silent.
Or sadly and ignorantly just unseen.

Not knowing, not hearing, not blending,
some eyes and ears sense nothing new.

Simply, unfortunately, just missed.
Unnoticed.

Through the magnolia, beyond
the listening lark upon the outside sill.

Triumphant in glorious hue, within,
the choir in the small chapel on the hill.

The souls upon the alley concrete.
The song of our Lord calling us all, each.

Sound of Light

Who shall we now see and *hear*?
The texture of the Voice, our Shepherd.
Not a voice of the past, but Alpha and Omega.

It reaches with presence, a chorus of angels.
Ongoing into the dark, as if hope in the light
is fire enough, like a floodlight with sound.

Light is more profound than earth's words.
It knows us. Sees us. Even through the obscurity,
walking upon the water, upon the horizon.

It meets us, is with us, on that very daily way,
this Way of Light, this Via Lucis.
An opus.

A beacon, as if where the new sun is lifted
with no defeat, through the thick parchment.
The runes reach out to us in Spirit. Even now

before night sky melts away.
The indelible vision yet to be fully seen
speaks emphatically even in all this blankness.

It speaks of that which is the very Light.
Calling each of us by name
to be alive in that Light the very same.

See a Choir of Angels

Even if we are alone
and seemingly forgotten,
we are not.

The Lord speaks with us.

Listen,
a back-and-forth dialogue
of prayer.

Listen,
sure as the most robust voice.

Listen,
the soul's heartbeat.

Open that heart.
Speak.

See the Risen Lord is here
to listen.

Bramble on the Cold Hill

Clarity of eternity is within the seed.
Heavenly made with heaven in the plan.
Leaves softly speak in the breeze.
Soon, reddened brittle,
all then fall with a whisper, buried
in snow at last with seed, fast asleep.

Allow the Maker
to sculpt away the stone,
the seed not to be found as a cold statue,
but glory of life as conceived.
See the undeniable truth as meant to be.
In you and all of life.

Trust and believe.

Soon to glisten in the melt of the sun.
Birds in nests branch to branch,
miracle of life is not happenstance.
We all can sing of Lord's mercy still.
And, even in the fray of life's disarray,
Love's continuance.

Persistence of Light

Even in the supposed silence of darkness,
even in a starless sky between the claps
of consonants, and in the resonant rumble

of persistence, a poetry. Calling. Steady
and sure, like the breezy rain, the headwind,
the peaceful beat upon the stern. We stop

to listen more closely to the voice of heaven,
ever near, calling in a wordless way
through the spoken Word. Not a roar

into night's end, but more. Waiting for us.
Lovingly calling to us.
To love.

Rapid Eye Movement

When of night, darkness grows wide.
We give in.
To faith.
Let us sleep and flicker in our peace.

May we be heightened by hope,
despite the muted roar of all the deep.
Hope reigns near the heart, at our being,
indelibly here for us to be seeing.

So much is taken for granted but
inner eyes delight in the truth.
We are made to trust heaven's light.
No matter the mountains of darkness.

Let us refine this refrain of our song,
its curl of clef and cadence all along,
to elevate the illustriousness of life.
And this way surrender to Light's hope.

We shall swim like dolphins,
and be emergent like the rising sun,
aside each other in a sea of morning light,
confetti in the glitter of our souls.

Love levels straight forward the way.
So it goes to trust in faith.
So it goes to believe.
Yes, yes. This is what love means.

Morning Walk

Still hills parked as if in a portrait,
we finally soften but do not melt away.
We then eagerly stand to face the east.

Hand in hand we now make our way
upon vacant asphalt and across seas
of broken glass amidst weeds.

Sun is unseen in the distance but heard
here as a call to action by the birds,
sure as unreadable signs rattle to speak

of our one human race.
There is a path we can go pole to pole
leaping across chasm.

This tightrope of life through the void,
this everyday leap, this everyday need
for trust is repeated day and day again.

It is settled simply by faith as we go.
All the way here to meet the rising sun,
the Risen Lord present in everyone.

Let us pray and listen again
for the Light's calling.
It lifts its song from within the sparrows.

And see how the Risen Lord walks with us.

windows on the way

stained
glass at a glance
reformed liquid sand
transparent and
heated quartz sand
silica soda ash and more
depending on the hues
above 3,090 degrees melt
into liquid cooled

and transformed not fully
amorphous sand
into a crucible
into a kiln
into all the light

melted sand into a mix
melted to be stirred
melted to be molten
the cooling process and
over time the annealing
a strength though delicate
apertures for the wise

so go all our eyes
even for the blind
to see Light
and to reveal Light
to see souls and skies

While on the Everyday Way

If headstrong, we might push forward, too often with blinding pride in our step. There is so much to lose. In the dark. On the road to Emmaus or anywhere, if our eyes are closed. We might even forget who we are, and Whose.

Meantime, the road directions are all around us. And on the GPS. On the common path, even in a stranger's face. And in the mirror. In the manger, if we are wise enough to see the star set before us, the pattern in scripture over the ancient course of ages, this very past moment. In the letters upon the bloodied parchment nailed high upon the wood. Everywhere. Everyday. The signposts old and written anew.

King of Radiant Glory

Through mercy
immeasurable,
we are never alone.

We are all friends,
no longer strangers,
fellow passengers
on the lambent way.

In each other, Who
shall we see?
In the eyes, Who
shall we recognize?

The Wise

Life is to live the Epiphany.
This, as we walk the everyday way.
Far from Christmas, yet ever near.
For Emmanuel is here. Everyday.

We followed yonder star here.
We are now amidst all the straw.
We are here, even in the cacophony,
the harmony, for each.

The Lord is here, everywhere,
near as a simple breathed prayer.
The Lord is here, loving our voice.
Gone is the darkness.

We present our gifts
more valuable than gold,
frankincense, and myrrh,
but our souls sunlit.

We Are Here

It is not yet apparent
what we shall become.

When that is finally visible,
face to Face with God,

O that we will be
as God wants us to be.

Intertwining
as our God-given selves.

Awe of that starts everyday
on the way.

Prayers Within Windows

We cannot comprehend even ourselves,
let alone the Lord to Whom we pray.
Love is far more than defining Divine,
more than just a fleeting blossoming.

It is joy despite all suffering.
It is giving it to the Lord.
It is receiving beyond our senses.
It is us, joyous on our daily way.

We are all that is life in a glorious refrain,
the doxology our inner eyes shall bring,
knowing the wonder we are made to be.
Joyous on our daily way.

See you, see me.
Yes, we know who we are within.
We are awakening in the starlight.
Joyous on our daily way.

There is a landscape to make wide.
We are to be the sunrise.
The Lord takes us each by the hand.
Joyous on our daily way.

Simple it is.
Like children at play.
Like hope of the new day.
Joyous on our daily way.

Wick Within the Wax

Tinder the thread.
More than between the ears.
The soul sings.
From deep within.
More than one's own voice.

Listen to the sun rise.
Yeast for the bread.
Unclog the ears.
Sound of somewhere birds
majestically near.

The most important part of a prayer
is the start.
The rest flows, loud as a candle.
O, that we may have a heart that hears.
O, that we may have a heart.

To know You
in the breaking of the bread.

In the Breaking of the Bread

Life
is more than a dream.

More than just a vision
or an unexpected vagary.

Bread is broken.
Hearts are open.

Love is action.
It cannot help but to be.

To nourish.
To feed.

So much to see,
to give, to share.

In the same way,
we are real

and are made to reveal
who we are.

And When the Wick Withers

Flame can incinerate,
yet also be earth's saving gift.

It can suffocate if we smother it.

It can run free, yet by grace,
peace by peace, enlighten.

Maker, what in us do you wish to ignite?

And, after this wick, what will be next?

Precious the gift of life.
But what shall last?

Though the wax may drop,
the way of the fire does not.

It can forever leap
like a flare cast.

Within Awe

Divine surpluses our line
of mortal minds as made,
and loves us.

Mercy secures us,
no matter the fear we might harbor,
fear of the unknown.

Love shall endure us,
and form us simply to love
one another.

And from this call of Love
that which calls us
to be nothing less,

we make our shared way.
Sent forth by the Light.
As Light.

Sunshine Upon Our Foyer

Even if now dormant, save for the memory,
or the glimmer of hope, we are.
And that enough goes vibrant.

Know us as such, even in cold darkness,
deep and ever present from before the seed.
An idea, created as a dream.

We know what we saw.
Light.

Despite all gloom.

We know we now see.

Ourselves as never the same.

Forever is next.
To be by the Maker's mercy, reality.
And then, vibrant green leaves breathe.
A life full, and ever grateful.

So go sparrows at an empty nest.
Gratitude for sky. To share.

Like Lilies Love Light

Our gratitude
is the recognizing
as best we humanly can,
Your face.
Thank You for being You.

Gratitude is our attitude.
And by Your grace,
toward You, our Savior,
with inner need without end,
we bend.

Walking Back From Emmaus

We are blessed on this path, step by step.
Eyes are opened as Isaiah had forecast.
Though darkness had covered the earth,
the Lord has now dawned His glory.
Yes, we have seen the Lord!
O the faces we now wear and share!

Yesterday's pain is outlasted by Love.
Love has cast away the darkness.
This Love, this act of God gathers
and lifts the world ever new.
His sacrifice for our souls, paid in full.
We are saved, and this we joyously see.
Out of the burdensome blight,
into the glorious delight of Easter day,
ever grateful we are to be in the light.

Death's emptiness is forever defeated.
And see, the Risen Lord is ever near,
in the breaking of the bread,
in communion with us here.

And see, He appears to us everywhere.
Walks with us, the valley of the living
on our same path twixt the cemetery trees,
through the skyscrapers and factories,
all along going to here, the shared way
where we belong.

Living Like Psalm 23

Love is with us.
The whole way.
Living as sung in Psalms.
Pasture in this valley is sweet
in all this Light.
Beyond time, but simply now.
Beyond place, but simply here.
Here where we are sheep
found
among the angels.
To be angels.

Acts of the Apostles

Each of us, every day.
On the everyday way.
In the Spirit, all that moves us,
moves all the universe.
This is us, supernatural beings.
Doing supernatural things.
All glory to God.

Each of us, every day.
Each, an everyday face.
Face to face on the way.
The imperfect
made perfect through grace.
Giving and forgiving.
Each of us, every day.

This is us surrendering.
This is us with joyful fate.
To be loved and loving.
Receiving mercy on the way.
Here, the Way of Light.
Seeing God.
Face to face.

Vibrant Field of Blossom

And together, the mosaic!

Love is happening.

The sound of colors, joyous,
everywhere in Christ's light
with so much to fully see.

In God we trust.

Faith of a child.
There is nothing else to need.
Nothing is more powerful
than to believe.

One by one by one…

Here, ever near.
A vibrant field of blossom opening.

Children
in the school playground playing.

Power of Peace

Shalom aleichem.

Here
in the City of Peace
and everywhere

across the verdant pasture,
not far away in some neverland
but here.
Near as heart to heart to heart.
Here.

We can fly for the olive leaf
and search for it everywhere
and it will be no sleight of hand.

Sky can fall into the seas.

Peace shall save us all.

Here
where we are.

Here
for us to now know firsthand.

Promised land.

In the palm of the Lord's hand.
Here.

This Way of Light

Signpost we can each be.
Each, a grateful sheep.
Each, aware of the lost.
The Lord's outstretched arm,
yes, we can be.

The sign of peace.

Puzzle Peace

We
reach
somewhere deep.

find ourselves,
and all the world,
every face a mirror.

We find ourselves
found.
Unfinished, yet perfect.

Jagged edges to the sky.
It all comes together
somewhere in every eye.

A rolled away stone.
The cosmos.
The gift of peace.

We reach forward.
Touch the stars.
So much room for mercy.

Peace Talks

We all empower peace
its voice.

How will we

speak?

How will we

listen?

In the sound,
Who shall we see?

Peace talks.
We all empower peace
its voice.

How will we speak?

How will we listen?

In the sound,
Who shall we see?

True Colors

Out of gloom and darkness,
even the eyes of the blind
shall see.

Seeing is believing,
so goes the cliché.
We are all blind

in ignorance
until the array of diversity
dispels the blank page.

Let us all be true,
with beams through us,
with light for each other.

To see the Risen Lord.

If only we believe
in what the good Lord sees
in us.

Of the Marks We Leave

We etch earth, often so creatively carving it
as if with hands and hammer of heaven.
We engrave, just by being us, leaving tracks

and they often crisscross. We err,
for our way is often one paved with mistakes.
Life takes legroom—lots of moving parts. And

new problems along the way. A problem
is a resolution waiting to rear its lovely head.
Yet, far too often, cruelly, we become numb.

And often see no one, even as we punch.
We lose sight even of ourselves.
In all the faces we share, what is our mark?

If image and likeness of the One,
why are we this way so imperfect?
Why would our Maker's face be so bereft?

Still,
when looking at those scars,
why is that face of the Lord so forgiving?

Prayer for Faith in the Dark

O Risen Lord,
blessed are we who do not see and yet believe.
This involves far more than the eye.

Many would be right, indeed, to be wary
of the physical eye, and even all the senses
except…

that which is formidable within.
O Risen Lord,
Fortify our inner eye, our compass of faith.

O Risen Lord,
You Who sees us, bless us with faith,
our Lord and our God.

O Risen Lord,
from the depth of Thy scars, from the dark,
enlighten our way.

Love Never Dies

We have nailed Love to the cross,
but are loved despite.
We have denied Love.
Have run to the dark so to hide.
But Love is the Light.

The mortal body dies.
This poem is not an elegy.
Not a cry.
Not a sorrowful lamentation,
nor a sobbing about demise.

But more so about what survives.

Without Faith, We Cannot Survive

Now that it is said, is it true?

Well, ask yourself this:
how to get out of bed?

How to put one foot before the next?
How to get by in between breaths?

Faith, the power to believe,
is more important than the air we breathe.

Without it, there is no letting go
breath to breath.

Without it, step by step,
the darkness overtakes.
We lose our sight in all our doubt.

See the sun. It rises.
It ushers in the new day.
Love the Maker of it.

There is so much we can brush aside,
even the darkness, if we had faith.
Even mountains, if they block the way.

Love Is to *See* and Believe

Some see themselves as hallowed and see only hollowness. Some see their god in their dead-end worldliness. Some may believe in a limited god, as only invisible.

The blessed aglow see God everywhere and believe. They know that face to face to face to face, all along the way, Christ is waiting to be seen. Even by the blind, those who trust their inner eyes. Blessed are those who have not seen, and yet still believe.

To *see* matters not so much to the eye, but to the epiphany within the soul.

Here we all are in front of our nearby mirrors, in each other's vast eyes, signpost by signpost by signpost. With each of us being God's image, Who do we see on our daily pilgrimage? In the scars, in the loveliness, Who do we *see*?

Wounds of the Living

How powerful life can be. How fragile! Why be troubled? It is this way for you and me, all of us on the way. In all our temporal needs as human beings, so much we may want. Yet, as sheep, nothing. We have all we need. Love exceeds the overflow of all wicker baskets.

Love is abundantly chromatic in its palette of peace. Still, yes, the wounds are real. Life is no early morning cartoon, but all day too often painfully real. Take within what is not a genie in a bottle for wishes to come true. But joy in what already is true. And real. Like me. Like you. Here upon the green valley, where sky turns its face to the light. Near as the Nativity is Good Friday. See, despite the inevitable travel of time, our physical beings are phenomenal wonders of a handmade Eden. And, formed in the womb, eternal, precious from conception, our innermost beings are complete.

As this miracle of walking on water has happened again and again, why be troubled? There is more to us than breakable skin. So, let us go forth to heal as we have been healed. And to treasure every soul's dignity within. To forgive as we have been forgiven. To die, as we have been given eternal life. Nothing of our doing. Except our surrendering. Our crosses and our wounds, we give it all. And we are blessed to receive the essence far superior to any fluorescence, simply the peace of the recurring present. Yes. Blessed.

Our Divine Lord knows us firsthand.

Moonrise Over the Sea

Still,
in fear of storms,
we sometimes forget the way.

In those unfortunate times,
         we fall in our blindness to see.
               Risen Lord, in that darkness
help us put forth our feet.
Enable us to step through the black mist
                     upon this lonely sea

and fully believe

You are the way.

No Need to Worry

Sun today
steps upon the Sea
of Galilee.

So, here we are,
another day
for miracles to be.

Wide the world
wherever we are,
step by step.

And look how far
we have walked
on water.

Living the Living

O, to be living the living with the Risen Lord and to cherish the
treasures of the deep. To allow the light to land upon this very
beach, and for all of us to look into each other's eyes and then
His. And to see what we may have thought to have been finite,
now simply infinity. For here He is, indeed, real in this given
grace. With us. Beyond death. Beyond all last breath.

We breathe. We are flesh and bone, and in communion. We
share our baked fish, freshly caught. Transported from the
netherworld upward, from the deepest sea, to wide upon our
eyes, here, now. No ghost, no fantasy, no wish, no figment to half
reminisce, but real presence. Real aroma. Real food to eat.
Touch our chests and feel the beat. See the rising of each new
and next breath.

Is this everyday miracle unbelievable?

We shall go living this way in our believing. Yes, even here,
especially here in our very everyday being where here at our
table we now say our grace.

Our Everyday Place

If only we remember this, even if the nets go empty and hope depletes. Even when we feel so ineffective in defeat. There is more to life than what we might think of as success. More than the net full of 153 large fish.

By the sea, an overflow of gifts. Not just the providence of this present breakfast but the sharing everyday of daily bread. In a very real and tangible way, this gift of sharing, with grace is us, face to face. With purpose.

And here is togetherness. Oneness. So it goes, and stays, this journey we share every day. Here as one, on our way.

Gathering of Stars

O Risen Lord,
You call us by name.

And now in all the shattered obscurity,
after all our devastated hopes, and fears,
we are strengthened and nourished.

We are empowered with the gift of faith.
And we know we can now set our nets.
We can set out our nets for Your purpose.

Here to the cosmos.

This togetherness is all of us, with You
on the Way of the Light.

To Shepherd Us

Even in the darkest of times,
the Lord is here.
The Source of light.
Always.
Everywhere.
To be with us.
To comfort us.
To save us.
To lead us.
To walk with us.
To talk with us.
To rise above the mourning.

Do You Love Me?

Why must I answer that?
Is it not known?

But before the crying crow,
I had denied all there is of Light.

And by the third time now asked,
maybe I realize the gift of mercy.

Love is the proper noun infinite.
Love is a verb, infinitely the same.

I know now how to answer.
In my smallness.
In my need.
In my gifted by God infinite way.
Time to feed the sheep.

To love, each is known.
And we all share this valley.

To love the Lord.

How infinitely blessed I am
to love Love.

Act of God, Act of Love

We are called to love.
See heaven here.
Heart to heart to heart.
We are not just angels above,
not in the mist of a mountain,
but upon the daily dirt path.
There is nothing we shall fear.
As sung in Psalms, we see light.
Amidst the ruin, upon a cross.
Darkness in our souls is erased
by the Lord's precious blood.
By act of God, we are loved.
For God is Love.
Blessed are souls to be believing.
By act of God,
in him we live,
and move and have our being.
By act of God, in the light
we are.

We are made to shine.

And Forth We Are Sent

Daily wars have layered scars upon scars. And yet, here still we are. We are all in need of mercy. We've heard Him say, seven times seven, the need to forgive. Yes, here we are with the need to be forgiven. And forth we are now sent. To forgive. This is our Way of Light to live. Peace is a path. Not just the stuff of angels, not just of the scintillating Divine, but of here where we mortals miraculously move and have our being. Let us not lose ourselves marveling at the power of the Peacemaker. Let us surrender and that way simply be.

Love Ascends and Stays

Shall we forever look upward
and wonder?

Shall the gleam inevitably dissipate?

Shall the darkness return,
sure as end of day?

Let us not disperse empty handed.

Rather,
let us go forth with our hearts full.

Love fits the soul.
Despite all overflow.

So goes the life-giving filament.
Now within.

Your Light Shows the Way

The world can be a difficult place.
Gravity hurts.
We may fall in our darkness,
nail down Your hands,
and yet,
You won't hold back Your sun.

Sky is wide to remind us
the depth of Your love.
You love everyone.
Within our hearts You provide light
so that we may now know paradise
near as here.

Sky Lanterns

This earth of our birth
cannot hold us down.
We are of heaven conceived.

Our hearts lift as if to beat,
as Easter's Love we speak,
as instruments sharing kindness.
Yes, where there is darkness,
Light.

Here we are, made to animate.
Life, ever lucent, unclouded,
we lift our prayers to heaven
as if to breathe,
by design as made from earth
to be

endlessly more than earth.

Sometimes It's Just Overcast

Sometimes
we suffer imperfect vision,
ever human.

Sometimes
angels remind us
the existence of the Divine.

Sometimes
we each need to be a sign,
an angel pointing the way.

Sometimes
we just have to remind ourselves
it won't always be drought nor rain.

Despite the mist of our eyes,
see, it is still there.
Here.

Be.

Light.

Presence of God

And life has its time of wait.
We keep vigil.
Never empty-handed.
Amidst the angels and saints,
with the Immaculate Conception,
with God here as Love.

Love is beyond time.

For Love is present and complete.
Ever near as here, even as it flows.
Here where we stand sure as sun.

Sun stands firm but runs to sea.
We are far more than what is of earth.
More,

as the flower is far more than dirt.

Every day is the same massive sun,
small in comparison
to the Love abounding for everyone.

Depth of Self

We have been given free will,
a phenomenal gift.
We have the freedom to believe.
Or to not believe.
Meantime,
outer space grows wider.

All along,
the Lord is waiting within.
Closer than any light speed
through the dark.
Hand out to lift away
the shadow.

In the depth
to the surface
we are not alone.
All of humanity is here.
We all share a Face.
The Lord is here.

O that we may see
the very Lord who seeks us
and meets us
in the day-to-day ruts
on these streets we erode.

Here within our souls.

Nimbus of Us

We can shadowbox the shadows and get lost in the difference in the gambit between partly sunny and partly cloudy and lose sight of ourselves even under shared umbrellas in the rain. Or we can take the bushels off our lamps, and let it be our City of Light. Yes, life is about those bushels and how to finally unveil ourselves. Our Lady is with us. All the saints. All holy souls. All the world, no matter the place. Even without words, I can speak to you, one by one. You can speak to me. And we can then see our poetry. Hello to every halo. And from within, welcome each gloriole. Cover not the candle. Put no lampshade upon the Miracle of the Sun. Know that God is in everyone. Waiting. Open our eyes ever wide, and see us emanate as we are, each a precious soul inside. One by one, all of us. One. Yes, let it be, City of Light. And, thus, we shall see ourselves as made to be.

We All Know Hope

We may not hold it, but we know it.
We know it especially
in the perceived absence of it.
When lost, there is so much to miss.
And how special it is when we have it.
It helps defeat all emptiness.

But it's not a carrot on a stick.
It's not folly, nor only a wish.
Hope is more than the vibrant false peak
to the weary climber.
It's more than virtual reality
in the pane of the glass to the fly trapped.

It's more than the sublime magazine ad
advertising something to possess.
It's even more than the next breath.
And the next.
It's in the breadth of this very moment.
We know it as we need to breathe.

We know it as a glowing gift to cherish.
Life has its clouds of darkness,
the feared hopelessness.
And yet, Light simply is.
Even in darkness, in heart ever within.
And so, hope exists, as if timeless.

Holy Spirit

God is.
Was.
Always shall be.
God is.
Now.
Here with us.

Take these hearts, Risen Lord.
Here where we are,
not hidden in a breathless tomb.
But Yours, in the light.
What is eternal is here, now.
Each heart spacious as the universe.

Despite agony, all the glory.
Despite poverty, wealth
far more than earth's mammon,
more than valueless 30 pieces of rust.
For the soul is invaluable.
Endless from within the womb.

And here we are,
radiant with each face,
for here is where You are.
We are each a representation of You,
each, from within,
the very precious awe of You.

Spirit, Breathe

Refresh these tired banners that bend
for You. Rapture all our flags and
give them life. Lift the grains of sand,

rippling day to night. Take us by the hand,
not to disarray but rather to Your divine design
upon the desert and upon the sea.

Spirit in the air and in our hearts, restrain
Your ever capable might. If You may,
You who command the dance of every flame,

rush and give music the song to its chime.
Brush mercifully and, at your authority,
ever kind, allow us, this humankind, to be

Your kite in flight.
And we shall gloriously fly
back to Your ever nearby loving hand.

And Who Are We?

How shall we be?

What if
the purpose of existence,
moment to moment,
now,
always is
simply this:

to be with and for
the good Lord
in every circumstance?

How then would we live?

Simply, extraordinarily,
as we are made to be.

Light.

We Are the Light of the World

We can phantom the future.
We can scan the past and see
all the sea,
all that we have walked across.

And now,
as all along, we are still here.
Not meant to be hidden.
But light to be shared.

Why?

It is the reason we are who we are.
It is the illumination of truth.
It is us in the Lord's image.
It is the Way of Light to enfold.

See
every moment a nearby epiphany.
The Risen Lord is by our side.
Holding our hand.

Lighthouse

Through black mist
we search for you, O God.
Far too often, we drift.
We lose ourselves in emptiness.
We thirst for your saving Divinity.
It is You, O Risen Lord, we need.

Without You, there is no light.

Help us to walk upon the water
toward that pedestal humbly
where you want us to be.

Each of us is unique.
Made that way to be.
Each of us is in need of community.
Made that way to be.

Facets of the priceless gem.
Us, no longer a distant *them*.
We are here as one, complete.
We give ourselves to You.

And then,
let that light cut through the night.
Use us, O Risen Lord.
Use us to be seen as You delight.

Inexhaustible

Here

to end of the earth,
see,

near
to nestled within,

the light,
an array of stars
of all that was,
all the universe,
all that is

love.

Lifts the sun.

And, yes,
see,

forever remains

truth

as darkness scatters.

Light Beams

Radiant the kaleidoscopic stream of light, luminous, full of life. And here is the universe within each, a spectrum known only through truth under the dabbing of stars at the reach.

Truth has presence, even if to others unseen. It is twined with Love. It is patient, persistent as the root of a tree. But closed minds are thick walls lost in blind spots seemingly impenetrable. We can blind each other, sadly, with our pride. We can choose ignorance and not light. Truth is indelible, yet our faces are easily fragile when camouflaged to hide. We can shut our hearts and lose what matters most. We can erase traces of light with our lack of love for ourselves and for others. Life without Love is darkness.

There is darkness for far too many. A Promised Land tantalizingly here but hidden. We are free, but what a regret to forget the light we are called to be. To not see a signpost to show the way. Nor one to be.

Thankfully, the Risen Lord is abundant in mercy. Always reaching, reaching for our epiphany, calling for our souls to see. We are made to be light beams of that mercy, refulgent, to show fullness of life despite the world's labels of emptiness. Despite the evil, the kind. To be the joy of existence as bestowed by heaven above. To be made full by the Lord, by Light to be light, by Love to be love.

Light-Bearers

In a world of darkness,
Light must not be hidden
but emblazoned.
Under the dog tag at the chest,
within the twine of all our need,
the bounding of faith,
in the fabric of the scapular,
we spark.

Sprung forth by vocation,
by that mission, a calling
to spread the thread of light,
we go as Christmas filaments
strung as fabric woven with fire,
that way bright, wired
to illuminate the earth and sky
with the Good News.

Light Carries Us

You've always held us
close to Your heart.

And gifted us
life's journey, free.

And see,
now the horizon
not only awaits us,
but also runs to us.
Opens wide its arms
for us.

It is You
Who longs for us,
Your children to hug.

Everything else
is superfluous.

Fireflies, Our Souls

Yes, from under the skin,
from within our skeletons,
our frames carry our flicker,
and we are more than the stars.

Just ordinary beings,
extraordinary we are.

We are all loved by God.

We read each other
as roadside signs reflective.
Intricate our design.
Spirit to fan our flame.

All along in the Light,
the most precious of all beings.

All along in the Light,
we are people of the Light.

And at the heart, the cloth,
the thread, the shared weave,
the wick, each and all,
a precious soul.

Ray of Light

Be.
As made to be.

Start
where you are.

Let go
to the incomprehensible,
as if ever simple,
the depth within,
the torch given.

Reach
and touch a star.

And, by gift of God,
you are
light.

Streams the Light

And here we are
in the luminance,
this tapestry of radiance,
this embroidery
of glimmering luminosity.

Here we are,
this spring of enlightenment.
You make us each a ray.
O Risen Lord, yes,
you make this of us.

You enlighten the way,
station by station, signpost
to signpost, this Via Lucis,
this immeasurable gift,
our daily joy,

this Way of Light.

Via Lucis

O Risen Lord, show the path of righteousness,
out of the darkness to the moment timeless.
Christ our Light, show the way.

O Risen Lord, enlighten us to truth
here on the Way of Light,
this our daily joy beyond all sacrifice.

O Risen Lord, we abide in You, our Shepherd.
And there is nothing, to fear, not even death.
Out of the blight of night, mercy, and salvation.

O Risen Lord, thank You for burning in us Love,
that which completes us,
that which we are called to embody for all.

O Risen Lord, You bring us perfect peace.
You are the same Holy Spirit Who embraced Paul,
the lives of yesteryear and to come, and now us.

O Risen Lord, light-bearers, let us be.
We are made by Your Light to be Your Light.
For all, let this shared poetry of prayer speak.

O Risen Lord, Who do we gloriously see?
You. Again, again, You show the Way of Light.
You are the way. Amen, Amen.

www.ingramcontent.com/pod-product-compliance
Lightning Source LLC
LaVergne TN
LVHW092022190726
843493LV00002B/548